How To Theme:

Understanding and Analysing the Connection Between Theme and Story for Writers And Students

AMY LAURENS

OTHER WORKS

SANCTUARY SERIES
Where Shadows Rise
Through Roads Between
When Worlds Collide (2018)

NON-FICTION
The 32 Worst Mistakes People Make About Dogs
How To Plan A Pinterest-Worthy Party Without
Dying or Losing Your Chill

INKPRINT WRITERS
How To Write Dogs
How To Theme

Find other works by the author at
http://www.amylaurens.com/books/

How To Theme:

Understanding and Analysing the Connection Between Theme and Story for Writers And Students

AMY LAURENS

Inkprint
PRESS

www.inkprintpress.com

Print ISBN: 978-0994523891
Ebook ISBN: 9781386724575

www.inkprintpress.com

National Library of Australia Cataloguing-in-Publication Data
Laurens, Amy 1985 –
How To Theme
104 p.
ISBN: 978-0994523891
Inkprint Press, Canberra, Australia
1. Creative Writing 2. English Literature—Themes, Motives 3. English Literature—Study and Teaching

First Edition: June 2018
Printed in the United States of America.

Cover design © Amy Laurens.

CONTENTS

INTRODUCTION

Theme.

Apparently, it's a scary word, one that sends students, readers and authors alike into fearful fits, remembering the Bad Old Days of high-school English. (And if this doesn't apply to you, congratulations! You'll still learn something from this book, you just get to skip the anxiety stage. And if you're still *in* high school, well, hopefully by the time you're done reading this book, English will seem a little less intimidating. We can hope, right?)

It's a shame, really, that so many English teachers end up inducing in their students fear of the very thing that makes stories stories, especially since we, as a profession, are generally some of the greatest story-lovers on the planet.

And okay, not all of us manage to terrify our students into quivering wrecks every time the T-word appears; some of us even actually manage to teach our students what theme is, and how to find it. I obviously believe wholeheartedly in the value of English teaching, and English teachers in particular—"obviously" because I am one.

But it is nevertheless an inescapable truth that many students have negative, overwhelming exp-

1

eriences in high school English, and if that's you, and all you're left with is a lingering sense of anxiety about what exactly a theme is, you're one of the lucky ones. Some students make it through high school English and never pick up a book again.

Heck. Some students make it *through* high school English without even picking up a book.

Another obvious statement: I think this is pretty sad. But what might surprise you is that the reason I think this is pretty sad is actually closely tied with this idea of theme. Let me explain.

Throughout this book, you'll find out that first of all, theme isn't as hard as you're afraid it might be; in fact, you've been doing it since you first began listening to stories, and your average seven-or-eight-year-old can be a relatively competent theme-spotter.

Secondly, you'll find out that theme is the part of stories that make them important to us as humans; themes are how stories teach us how to human.

That's why I think it's pretty sad that some people never read again after high school English—because if you don't have stories to help you learn how to human, you either need darned good mentors in your life (which is possible, though less and less so as contemporary western society fragments us into smaller and smaller units), or you have to figure it all out for yourself.

Which, okay, there's a time and a place for experiential learning; some things you just have to learn by doing them yourself. But how to navigate heartache? How to empathise with people different from ourselves? How to keep our heads above water when everything around us seems to be pulling us down? Stories can teach us these things. We don't *have* to go it alone.

So it's pretty sad that a profession notionally dedicated to teaching people to love and value stories (i.e., us English teachers) is often the profession responsible for turning people off stories altogether—though usually that 'turn off' is limited to written stories, since visual stories (like movies and TV shows) are more pervasive, easier to digest, and, generally speaking for the average member of the human population, faster to consume.

Which brings me to another important point: themes aren't just for novels. I'm very deliberately using the term 'stories' here, because if it's a story, it has themes, and that applies to *all* stories, in *all* media: novels, short stories, TV shows, films. You name it. If it's a story, it has a theme. If it's a story, it's teaching us how to human.

Some stories do a better job of teaching than others, of course, but that doesn't change the fact that what I'm going to talk about here is as easily applicable to your favourite movie as it is to your favourite book—or that book you're writing, if that's you. You'll see that in the examples.

Theme also applies to every genre of story. It can be tempting, thanks to some of your historical English teachers (or current ones, if you happen to be a student right now), to imagine that theme is solely the domain of stuffy, literary novels designed to make your brain hurt.

Now, I've nothing against a good stuffy, literary novel (though I do have a distinct preference for ones with something uplifting to say about humanity—there's enough pain and agony in the world to make me feel hopeless without my fiction trying to tell me that as well—and you'll realise by the end of this book that this statement is almost *exclusively* about themes), but a novel—a story—doesn't have to be stuffy and/or literary in order to have a theme.

Every story has a theme.

Every story has *multiple* themes.

(This is one of those things that people who prefer the black/white aspect of high school maths often resent about high-school English. It also makes it harder to be good at English without really engaging, because you kind of actually *have* to have an opinion in order to have something to say.)

And, interestingly enough, different genres tend to have different clusters of related themes. An integral part of romance, for example, is the happy ending—and guys? *That's related to the themes.*

Okay. Enough introduction. Gird your loins, refill your coffee cup, grab your pen, your enthusiasm, and a good, stout leash for your anxieties: it's time to analyse theme.

PART ONE

Before we get to talking about what exactly a theme is, it helps to have a refresher about things like theses. If you're super comfortable already with the idea of a thesis statement, let me give you the potted summary right here:

Theme is to fiction as thesis is to non-fiction.

Or, even more simply:
The theme is the point of the story.

If you're happy with that, feel free to jump ahead to chapter three. Otherwise, stick around and we'll do a quick refresher.

CHAPTER ONE

Our starting point is this:

Everything is a text.

This, as I would say to my students, is a text right now, a little more obvious to *you* because you are reading literal words I have written, but no less applicable to the students in my classroom, sitting in front of me, listening as I create a verbal text.

Everything is a text: that ad flashing on the side of your screen, this book you're reading, that TV ad playing in the background... (Wait what, people watch TV with ads still? Yeah, yeah, I'm stuck in the dark ages, I know). The song you're listening to, the advertising poster you drive past on the way to work or school, the conversation you just had with the person next to you.

Everything is a text, and these days, as an Australian English teacher, I'm pretty much expected to be across all of these text types. What a good thing there are a lot more similarities than there are differences!

So, the next point is this:

All texts have a point.

See? I told you this would be easy. The point of this book, for example, is to convince you that theme is easy and accessible, and that knowing about it will enrich both your reading and your writing experiences; in short, I'm trying to tell you that theme is worth paying attention to, and that it won't break your brain to do so.

The point of an ad, generally speaking, is to convince you to buy something—unless the ads are produced by the government, or a non-governmental organisation (like a charity), in which case the point is often to change your behaviour, or convince you to donate money to something.

The point of songs varies widely, but layered in on top of the point of the lyrics is the *emotional* point of the music: music is supposed to make you *feel*.

Conversations vary widely in their purposes, too. Just in the last hour I've had a conversation where the point was conveying information about a block of a land; a conversation wherein I tried to convince the two-year-old that it really was time to go to sleep; and a conversation wherein the point was conveying gratitude for a brunch my family attended. In point (!) of fact, the latter wasn't even a conversation: it was a text message. Because yes, obviously, text messages are a type of text too, and they too have a point.

And in fact, it's even possible for 'no point' to be the point: I've had plenty of silly, giggly, meandering conversations with friends—usually late at night, hyped on sugar and short on sleep—where the entire point of the conversation was simply entertainment.

When you get to the stage where 'green cup' makes everyone explode with laughter, you know you're well beyond reason, but the statement 'green cup' still had a point: I can't even remember who it was that said that any more, but I do remember the mood, the tone it conveyed, the idea that we were all tired and silly and illogical but that we were these things together. In this context, 'green cup' was relatively empty of *literal* meaning (wow, yes, you're right, that is in fact a green cup; so observant of you), but rich, in context, with *emotional* meaning, and so all that emotional meaning *became* the point of that short, apparently-ridiculous text.

Also, you can create a point by accident. Have you ever had someone take something you said or wrote entirely the wrong way, leaving you blinking in shock, going, "But that's not what I *meant!*"?

Yup. Congratulations: you are such an expert point-maker that you make points without even realising you're doing it. This is going to be important later on, so tuck it away in your memory banks for future reference.

To recap:

Everything is a text. All texts have a point. Even the ones that seem like they don't,

because if you're intending to be pointless, well, you're still intending something, so the point is to be pointless. (Paradoxes, we can has them.) **You can also create a point accidentally.**

Now, for whatever reason, figuring out what the main point of non-fiction is seems much easier for people than figuring out what the main point of fiction is. Probably, this is because we feel safe relying on logic:

The point of a recipe is to tell you how to cook the item. The point of a dictionary is to define words. The point of an essay is to discuss such-and-such a concept (say, key themes in *Romeo and Juliet*). The point of a news article is to tell you what happened. The point of a magazine opinion piece is to convey the opinion of the writer. The point of an ad is 'This product is amazing enough that it's worth spending x number of dollars on it'.

Sometimes, we have fancy words to describe these 'points':

The point of an ad is often a <u>call to action</u>—the action the ad-makers actually want you to take after seeing the ad.

The point of a (non-fiction) paragraph is the <u>topic sentence</u>.

The point of an essay is the <u>thesis</u>.

The point of a story is the <u>theme</u>. (See what I did there?)

If you're feeling comfortable with this analogy, go ahead and skip on to chapter three now. If you'd like a bit of a refresher about what a thesis statement is (the point of an essay), continue onwards to chapter two.

(This is practically a choose-your-own-adventure, isn't it?)

CHAPTER TWO

Wait, what's a thesis* again?

Remember, thesis is singular, theses is plural.

If it's been a while since you last wrote an essay, or if you've somehow been writing essays all this time without understanding the concept of a thesis, let me break this down for you real quick.

The thesis of your essay is your main point, your key argument, the basic idea you are trying to convey. It's (hopefully) the first sentence or two of your essay, and it neatly sums up your argument.

The key to doing this well, of course, is to actually have a point that you're trying to make. It's all to easy to assume that because you're not supposed to write about your opinion in an essay, you're only allowed to be 100% factual. And I mean, *yes*, you're supposed to be factual, but the English analytical (or literary, or critical, pick your term, they all mean the same thing) essay is fundamentally a persuasive beast dressed up in objective clothing.

The bit that divides so many people in their opinions about English is the fact that there are multiple right answers (Because theme! More on this later), so essentially what you are trying to do in an analytical essay is prove that your answer is the best possible answer to the question. It's not your opinion of the text (no one actually cares that you hated the novel, sorry), but rather your interpretation of it that matters (Did Hamlet off everyone because madness, or because he was just a melodramatic jerk? Was Macbeth solely responsible for the immorality of his own actions, or does Lady Macbeth share some of the blame too?). So in order to craft a good thesis, you actually need to know what point about the text you're trying to make, and then convey that succinctly in a sentence or two.

(Incidentally, a good thesis, which creates a driving sense of purpose throughout the text, is the difference between a competent essay and a really good one.)

Let's have a look at some examples of theses.

Through the characters of Gwen and the Campers, Gow demonstrates throughout the play *Away* that mistrust of those different to us is absurd, and is rooted in ignorance.

Through the characterisation in his novel *Fahrenheit 451*, Bradbury suggests that the ability to think our own opinions openly with out fear of persecution, harassment or discrimination is integral to constructing our individual identities.

The novel *Jasper Jones* by Craig Silvey demonstrates through Charlie's journey that while moral duality is often demonstrated by adults in authority, it is never demonstrated by people who have truly 'grown up'.

You'll note that each of these thesis statements include three elements:
- <u>What</u> the author is talking about
- <u>How</u> this is seen in the text
- <u>Why</u> this is actually significant (or as I like to ask my students, 'Who cares?')

Incidentally, these are the holy trinity of English questions, the triad core around which all English literary analysis revolves. Any time you are asked to 'analyse a text', remember to cover what, how and who cares, and you're on safe ground.

Let's break some of those theses down to show you how this works:

1) Through the characters of Gwen and the Campers, Gow demonstrates throughout the play *Away* that mistrust of those different to us is absurd, and is rooted in ignorance.

<u>What</u>: We're talking about the idea of mistrusting people different to us, as shown in Gow's play *Away*.

How: This idea is developed through the characters Gwen and 'the Campers'.

Why: Gow is suggesting that mistrusting people different to us is absurd; it's rooted in ignorance, and isn't an ideal way to lead our lives. Gow is making a comment here about how we should actually live our lives, and the thesis recognises that something in this play is relevant to life outside the text.

2) Through the characterisation in his novel *Fahrenheit 451*, Bradbury suggests that the ability to think our own opinions openly without fear of persecution, harassment or discrimination is integral to constructing our individual identities.

What: The ability to think freely (or, the ability to live without censorship) in *Fahrenheit 451*.

How: This is explored through the characterisation in the novel.

Why: Bradbury is suggesting that this freedom is actually necessary in order for us to create our own identities; again, the author is making a point that is relevant to life outside the text.

3) The novel *Jasper Jones* by Craig Silvey demonstrates through Charlie's journey that

while moral duality is often demonstrated by adults in authority, it is never demonstrated by people who have truly 'grown up'.

<u>What</u>: Moral duality in *Jasper Jones*.

<u>How</u>: Charlie's journey.

<u>Why</u>: While it's possible for adults to be morally dualistic, actual, mature grown-ups are not; there's a difference between 'being an adult' and 'growing up'.

If you're happy enough with this, feel free to move on to chapter three now. But if you'd like to consolidate your understanding even further, have a look at the sample introduction below to see some thesis statements in context.

In each instance, you can see that the thesis statement clearly outlines the main argument of the essay, which is then supported by (usually) three key pieces of evidence, or parts of the proof, before then restating the point for clarity, or building on it to make very clear how this idea impacts life outside the text.

(English is actually really logical when you break it down, despite how it might feel. It's just the opposite of maths: you start with the answer, and then provide your working out to prove how you got there. A paragraph is just a maths problem in reverse—answer, show your working out, then repeat your answer to conclude. Ta da!)

The novel *Jasper Jones* by Craig Silvey demonstrates through Charlie's journey that while moral duality is often demonstrated by adults in authority, it is never demonstrated by people who have truly 'grown up'. While initially Charlie is ignorant of the moral duality rampant in his community, his relationship with Jasper exposes him to the cruel reality of racial discrimination and the dual standards people are willing to apply. This is further exposed by Charlie's relationship with Jeffrey Lu, and the discrimination Jeffrey faces in his efforts to join the cricket team. However, moral duality is best demonstrated by Charlie's relationship with his own mother, who demonstrates most clearly the idea that growing older does not necessitate growing up. Through Charlie's growing understanding of the experiences of these three characters, the novel clearly presents the idea that morals and ethics should be upheld regardless of the situation, and that this is a prerequisite for being a grown-up, contributing member of society.

There are a couple of things that I would change about this introduction still—I'm not claiming it's perfect—but it does demonstrate the idea that you have a thesis statement that answers what, how and who cares, then you have the three key ideas you'll discuss in your paragraphs, and then a concluding sentence for the paragraph.

Here's a slightly more complex introduction, in response to the question, "Even when texts seek to challenge some gender stereotypes, they ultimately reinforce others. To what extent is this true for *Jasper Jones?*":

Throughout Craig Silvey's *Jasper Jones*, violence is shown to be an inextricable part of stereotypical masculinity; however, Charlie's shift from seeing one's physicality as the primary source of power, to believing in one's integrity as the ultimate source of personal power, does suggest that it is possible to rise above this. Thus, superficially, this novel is an exhortation to shun society's stereotypes (part-icularly violence) in favour of developing empathy in order to help those in need, and showing integrity above all else. Upon deeper examination, however, the text reveals many contradictions. Despite his journey towards self-acceptance, Charlie still buys into the need to appear classically 'masculine' like Jasper, idolised by Charlie as the epitome of masculinity. However, Jasper is hardly an ideal to aspire to: alone, ostracised, and living in abject poverty. Even Jeffrey Lu, Charlie's charming and affable sidekick, becomes less clear on closer inspection: although he is obviously intended as the 'Superman' figure of the text, proclaiming nothing to fear and no fears worth having, in actual fact there is plenty in his life that needs overcoming, and it is only because he endures his trials with such apparent abandon that we care for him at all. Thus, although the message of the text regarding masculinity is clearly that men should develop and embrace their own identities, striving always to act with integrity, nonetheless there are difficulties inherent in many of the male characters that, while breaking down some masculine stereotypes, nevertheless reinforce many others.

This introduction is much more complex than the first one because the question is correspondingly complex (and again, it's not perfect!). The question is asking you to look at the ways in which the text both challenges some stereotypes, and reinforces others, so you need to do a bit more groundwork to set the scene for your thesis in order to convincingly prove your point. You can still see the general structure there, though: a two-part set-up for the thesis, the three key points for discussion (Charlie, then Jasper, then Jeffrey), and finally the summing up, restating the thesis statement clearly in response to the question with consideration for the influence of this idea on life outside the text.

So there you have it: the basics of a thesis statement, which is just the fancy name for 'the point of your essay'.

(BONUS! If you go back and have a look at all those 'Why' statements... Guys? *They are the themes of the texts!*)

CHAPTER THREE

Okay, so now that we've established the groundwork, we can get down to the nitty-gritty of why you're actually here: figuring out what theme is.

I said at the end of chapter one that people often find it easier to divine the point of non-fiction; this is because it's often stated clearly and specifically in the text itself. It's easy to tell the point of a well-written essay, because it's in the first one or two sentences—it's the thesis statement. (See chapter two if that's confusing.)

But what most people don't realise is that fiction often states its point outright as well!

Have you ever gone to GoodReads or Instagram or Pinterest or somewhere, and seen a quote that someone has pulled out of a book?

Have you ever typed up a quote yourself (whoa, the commitment), or taken a photo of one, or reposted, repinned, reblogged, or otherwise re-consumed a quote someone else uploaded?

Even if you haven't, you do get that this is a Thing that people do, right? Saving their favourite quotes from books and movies?

Yes?

Okay, good. Because Imma let you in on a little secret here, right now.

Ready to be blown away?

Chances are really, really high that the quote you saved/saw/pinned/regrammed/reblogged/whatever *directly states the theme of the story it came from.*

You don't believe me, do you.

Okay, let's try some examples.

...Wait. Before we do, I need to say something really, really important here:

The theme is never just one word.

'Love' is not a theme. 'Identity' is not a theme. These are concepts, topics, ideas—not themes.*

* I mean, you'll hear people say this all the time, and I'm even guilty of saying it sometimes (okay, class, today let's discuss the theme of love in Romeo & Juliet*!), but it's shorthand. It's not accurate. Themes must be a full sentence, because...*

These one-word descriptors *can't* be a theme, because theme is the point of a text, and the point of something isn't 'love', it's 'Love is a magical thing that can transform even the worst situations'; it's 'I love you'; it's 'Love is worth fighting for'; it's 'Love can transcend the barriers of time, space, and/or culture'. Theme is 'Self-sacrifice is the highest form of love'.

Theme isn't just 'love'.

See how all these are *statements* that say something *about* love? This is what I meant at the end of the introduction about needing to have an opinion; it's not that you need to have an opinion about the text itself (unless you're writing a book report or a movie review, no one cares if you liked the story or if you hated it), but you do need to *interpret* it.

You need to engage with what the text is *talking about*, not just at the plot and character level, but at the *meaning* level. What is this text saying *about life*, or some aspect of it? (Cunningly, those of you who read chapter two will also note that this is the 'why' or 'who cares' part of the thesis statement—you can go back and have a look at what I wrote for each of those 'why' sections, and you'll discover that each one of them is a theme.)

So. We know that 'literary' novels have themes:

"Terror made me cruel."
Wuthering Heights, Emily Bronte

What is Bronte saying here? Well, in *Wuthering Heights*, Bronte suggests that terror has the ability to make a person cruel. (Or, 'that cruelty is often rooted in fear'.)

"It's much better to do good in a way that no one knows anything about it."
Anna Karenina, Leo Tolstoy

Tolstoy, in his novel *Anna Karenina*, suggests that it is better to perform good acts in such a way that no one else knows anything about them.

"Life appears to me too short to be spent in nursing animosity or registering wrongs."
Jane Eyre, Charlotte Bronte

In *Jane Eyre*, Bronte suggests that there are better uses for our limited time than keeping records of wrongdoing.

"No man, for any considerable period, can wear one face to himself and another to the multitude, without finally getting bewildered as to which may be the true."
The Scarlet Letter, Nathaniel Hawthorne

In *The Scarlet Letter*, Hawthorne cautions that living a duplicitous life ultimately leads to a confused identity; we eventually become that which we pretend to be.

Okay. We get it. Literary novels state their themes outright in quotes.

But look! Popular texts do the same thing:

"Becoming fearless isn't the point. That's impossible. It's learning how to control your fear,

and how to be free from it."
Divergent, Veronica Roth

What is Roth suggesting here? In *Divergent*, Roth suggests that while it is impossible to completely eradicate fear, by learning to control our fears we can be free from them.

"You don't get to choose if you get hurt in this world... but you do have some say in who hurts you. I like my choices."
The Fault In Our Stars, John Green

In *The Fault In Our Stars*, Green suggests that while pain and heartbreak are inevitable, we have some measure of control in choosing who we allow close enough to hurt us, and that the joy brought by these relationships makes the pain worthwhile.

"No one ever made a difference by being like everyone else."
The Greatest Showman, directed by Michael Gracey

The Greatest Showman suggests that it is important to embrace what makes us unique if we wish to make a positive impact on the world.

"Do. Or do not. There is no try."
The Empire Strikes Back, directed by George Lucas

Through the character of Yoda, *The Empire Strikes Back* suggests that life consists only of failure or success, without any grey area in between.

"You say having feelings makes me weak, but you're weak for hiding from them."
Bodyguard of Lies (*The 100*, season two), directed by Uta Briesewitz

Through the character of Clarke, *Bodyguard of Lies* suggests that true strength lies in acknowledging our feelings, rather than denying them.

"In times of crisis, the wise build bridges, while the foolish build barriers."
Black Panther, directed by Ryan Coogler

Black Panther suggests that it is better to seek connections and partnerships when we are in trouble than it is to shut people out.

See? Pull-quotes from stories are usually thematic. Your subconscious totally knows how to spot theme, even if you can't consciously articulate that yet. So now we just have to learn how to make all that knowledge conscious.

Relax. It's going to be so easy.

CHAPTER FOUR

I'm going to give you a quick exercise I use in class to teach this. It involves reading a short fable, and then telling me what the moral of the story is. (In fact, if you grew up on the stereotypical western fable diet, you don't even need to read it: it's just the hare and the tortoise, after all.) Below is my own retelling of 'The Hare and The Tortoise'. Have a read, and then think about what the moral is.

Once upon a time, there was a hare, and there was a tortoise. The hare liked to run very fast. He ran to the hill. He ran to the tree. He ran home again.

But running by himself wasn't entirely satisfying. He wanted a partner to run with—someone to race. So one day, the hare challenged the tortoise to a race (all the other animals were currently avoiding him, as they were annoyed at him for constantly running at them, near them, or over them).

The tortoise, being a genial sort of fellow, agreed, and the time and date were set for the race.

On the day of the race, all the animals turned out to watch: the raccoon was there, and the badger, and even the bilby who was visiting internationally. They waved their little flags and cheered as the sun beamed down on the starting line.

Behind the starting line, the hare jumped and skipped and stretched, warming up in preparation for his amazing racing debut.

The tortoise watched quietly for a moment, turned around so he was facing a nice shrub, and closed his eyes.

The hare paused to stare in wonder. "Aren't you going to get ready?" he said.

"I am," said the tortoise.

The hare shrugged, bewildered, and went back to his acrobatics.

Before long, the crowd had gathered and it was time to start the race. The deer held the starter's acorn in her mouth, high above the heads of the hare and the tortoise. The hare tensed on the starting line, muscles taught, gathering for the leap.

The tortoise shuffled absently.

The deer let the acorn drop.

Eyes watched it fall intently — the crowd's, the deer's, the hare's.

The acorn dropped in the dust.

The hare exploded from the start line in a flurry of fur, and was gone around the first corner before the crowd had time to blink.

The tortoise gave a little sigh, and began plodding down the track, tuning out the scoffing of the other animals. (Bet you regret this now, don't you, Tortoise! I told old Jonny you were an idiot for trying this. Yah, is that the fastest you can go? My fleas run faster than you do!)

The sun beat down, as the sun is wont to do, and the air grew uncomfortably hot and steamy. Nine-tenths of the way down the track, the hare panted to a halt, gasping and clutching at the stitch in his side. *Where the flying flea circus is that tortoise?* he thought to himself (it being rather difficult to think to other people). *Never mind, I'll have a rest.*

The finish line was in sight, after all, and the tortoise was decidedly *not* in sight, and the sun was hot, and the air was thick and heavy, and oh look, right here was a tiny trickle of a stream, and if the hare stretched just right, he could wet the tips of his ears and oh, it was so refreshing. He sprawled in the grass and watched as a bee buzzed around the cloud-coloured blossoms on the bush above him.

Bzzzzzzz went the bee.

Zzzzzzzz went the hare.

Meanwhile, the tortoise was still plodding away, one slow, careful, laborious step after the other. He also was hot and thirsty, and it looked as though he was crying, but that is only because that's how tortoises sweat, and not because he was feeling particularly disheartened. In fact, as he crested a small rise, he felt *quite* heartened, because there ahead was the finish line, and there to his left, asleep beneath a bramble bush by a little soak, was the hare, twitching and mumbling in his sleep. A small smile tugged on the tortoise's mouth, and he headed through the last, dusty stretch of path toward the line drawn on the ground in the dirt.

As his feet scuffed the line and the animals broke out in cheers, a grey squirrel came bounding up. He lay a small wreath of flowers over the tortoise's neck, and danced in the dirt, clasping his hands before him. "But the hare is so much faster than you!" the squirrel cried. "However did you win?"

"Ah," said the tortoise in a voice that would have been annoyingly smug if it weren't for the fact that the hare was even more annoying, "the hare may be fast, but he is arrogant. He thought he was guaranteed to win, and so he didn't try his best. I, on the other hand, am slow, but I am persistent, and you'll find that in the end, the slow and steady win the race."

Okay, so that's the story,* for those of you who haven't heard it before or needed a refresher.

* *I mean* sort of. *The* shape *of it is right. I probably might have, um, embellished a few things. But it's still 'The Hare and The Tortoise', okay?*

So now my question for you is, what's the moral of this story? Take a second to think about it before you turn the page. If you've bought this book in paper, you could even (gasp) use the margins to write your answer, or a couple of answers, before turning over. (Only do this if it's your book though, obviously. Librarians and book collectors get cranky if you write in their books.)

If you are a relatively average human being (which is in no way an insult in this context, I promise), you'll have written (or *thought*—I know 99% of you did not write anything down) something like one of the following:

Slow and steady wins the race.

A good work ethic wins in the end.

Don't sleep on the job.

Don't be cocky.

If you identified something like any of the above, congratulations! (If not, just sit tight for a couple of paragraphs; I got you covered.) You just conclusively proved to yourself that you are an expert theme finder!

What? you say. *All I did was figure out the moral of the story!*

Yes. That is exactly right. **Because the moral of the story is the theme.**

And remember: **The theme is never, ever just one word.**

You'll also notice something else important: these statements are all comments on how we should live our lives, or ways to live a better life; these statements are offering advice and guidance, opinions on how we should live.

This is why themes are important, and why stories are able to teach us how to human.

Now, if you *didn't* identify something like the morals (themes) above for the hare and the tortoise story, take a moment right this minute to go back and reread the story so you can see how we arrived at these ideas. If you didn't get it, that's perfectly okay. It just means you need to practise the basics a little more before moving on.

Go on. Go reread the story, and think about how I figured out each of the 'moral of the story' statements.

I am literally going to wait right here while you do.

...

...

...

Okay. Done?

Promise?

I'm trusting you here.

So, especially if you struggled a little with this activity, but *even if you didn't,* I highly recommend browsing online through Aesop's fables or suchlike, and practising identifying the moral of each story. Not only will you get better at quickly identifying the moral of each story (the theme, remember), the whole exercise will also reinforce to you what I said about stories stating their points outright, and you'll probably start to notice a pattern: a lot of fables *do* state their theme outright, and a lot of them do it *near the end of the story.*

As it turns out, this advice holds across most story types; whereas in an essay or similar piece of non-fiction you look at the first line to figure out the point (the thesis), in a story, you look at the ending. And if you happen to be consuming a story that doesn't neatly lay out the theme for you in a quotable quote (ha), the ending is where you'll find the keys to unlocking the point of the story.*

Incidentally, most commercial films follow the same standard structure or pattern (which varies a little by genre but remains pretty consistent nevertheless). A key part of this pattern (called 'beats') is the 'statement of theme' beat, which happens right up front in the second scene. If you're paying attention, this is where a character—usually not the main character—will either make a statement or ask a question that turns out to sum up the main theme of the film.

CHAPTER FIVE

So you know now that one way to find the themes of a text is to look for 'quotable' bits, and another way is to see if it's stated in the ending somewhere. But what do you do if the theme isn't actually ever stated outright? (Hint: sobbing in despair is not the answer.)

Well, to find the theme of a text that doesn't helpfully state it outright for you, we need to look at both the characters, and the ending.

(Endings provide important clues for you about a story's theme mostly because this is where we find out which characters we're supposed to pay attention to, so really we're just looking at characters.)

Some helpful hints.

Look at the ending. Which characters end well? Sometimes, this means that the character gets a happy ending. Other times, however, the character themself might end sadly (dead, for example) but might succeed in getting what they wanted (they died, sure, but they saved their family by doing so).

So stop and think for a moment about which characters it seems like the story wants us to side with. I'm going to shorthand by calling these the good characters, even though they can actually be totally immoral; 'good' here just means 'the characters the story wants us allied with'.

Now do the opposite: who ends 'un-well'? They might get a literal sad ending, or they might just fail to achieve that thing they've been striving for, or they might succeed, only to find it was the worst thing in the world (I mean, Jafar gets what he wants in *Aladdin*, but I think we can all see that wishing himself into genie-hood wasn't exactly 'ending well'). I'm going to shorthand these characters as the 'bad characters', noting again that this has nothing to do with their actual morality.

The reason it's important to identify this is because generally speaking, a text suggests to us that we should do as the good characters do, and avoid doing as the bad characters do. And remember, if a text is commenting on what we should or shouldn't do in our own lives—that's theme.

(Jafar: Think through the consequences of your actions. Don't be a monumental, power-hungry jerk. Addictions to power never end well. Phenomenal cosmic power often results in itty-bitty (emotional) living spaces. Etc.)

So. You've done that, and we know which characters we're supposed to identify with, and which ones we're supposed to reject.

Now we need to examine the journey these characters go on to see what they learn along the way, because the lessons the characters learn? Yup, that's theme.

There are a few helpful questions you can ask yourself when thinking about a character's journey.

- What is the character like at the beginning of the story?
- What is the character like at the end of the story?
- What changed? What did they have to learn to be or do in order to get to the end?

(If you're looking at the 'bad characters', you can also ask, "What did they fail to learn that led to their downfall?")

Sum up that change in a nice, generally-applicable sentence, and you have a theme. In *Zootopia*, Judy Hopps started the story thinking that she knew everything and could tackle anything on her own. By the end, she's realised that she has blind spots too, and has learned some humility—as well as how to work as part of a team.

What changed in her attitude? Arrogance changed to humility, independence to team work.

Summing those up in generally-applicable sentences, we get:

Even when you think you're well informed, you don't know everything and you're still subject to bias.

(Or, even more simply, humility is preferable to arrogance.)

Even competent people need a team to support them in their work.

The other helpful thing to do is to look for key moments of failure and triumph for the character, and try to figure out why they failed or succeeded.

In *Harry Potter*, the darkest moment of the whole series is the end of book five (or movie five, either way), *The Order of the Phoenix*, where Harry realises that his visions were wrong, that Voldemort was deliberately luring him to the Ministry of Magic, and as a result of this, his godfather is killed. Given that one of Harry's key motivations throughout the series is to protect the people he loves (theme alert!), this is a failure of epic proportions: his one remaining relative who loves him is now gone, and it's almost entirely Harry's fault.

Why did he fail so direly here? Because he thought that he alone was capable of keeping his loved ones safe. Because he didn't trust the adults in his life to be competent and well informed. Because he allowed his own sense of importance (in being the only one privy to Voldemort's thoughts) to outweigh the explicit instructions of his mentor (though, granted, Dumbledore had been a head-master for long enough that he ought to have known better than to tell a teen to do something without a reason, and actually expect them to do it). Let's pull some themes out of that:

To keep your loved ones safe, it is necessary to sometimes trust others.

You are not the only competent person in the universe.

It is important to trust those who have proven themselves trustworthy.

Just because you don't know the reason behind something, doesn't mean it's not the right thing to do.

No one is so special that they can't make mistakes.

So much for failures; now what about successes?

Harry's ultimate success is at the end of the series, when he willingly sacrifices himself for the safety and protection of his loved ones, so that Voldemort can be finally made mortal and the world can be rid of his evil for good. Harry walks into Voldemort's glen, expecting full well that he will die, only to discover that, first of all, death is not the end, and second of all, neither is this the end for him. He rises again, but because he had died, Voldemort is now mortal and able to be vanquished, and not a single person at Hogwarts is able to be killed by Voldemort or his followers—a great triumph indeed. So, some themes:

Self-sacrifice is the highest form of love.

Love protects those we love. (Or, love has protective power.)

Courage is rewarded. (Harry is courageous as he expects to die, and his noble actions are rewarded—he returns to life.)

To rid the world of evil, good people must be willing to make sacrifices.

Death is not the end, and we should not live our lives in fear of death (as Voldemort does).

Let's wrap this up with a quick look at how we can develop themes from 'bad characters' and their failures. Voldemort is an easy example here, given he keeps metaphorically bashing his head up against the stumbling block of Harry time and time again during the series. He constantly underestimates what Harry is capable of, and at one point Dumbledore even points out his major weakness: he doesn't understand love (possibly *can't* understand it, given he was conceived under the effects of a love potion) and so refuses to take its power seriously. Let's thematise:

Don't underestimate your enemies/rivals.

Don't underestimate the power of something just because you don't understand it.

Love really does have power, and if you can't understand that, you're doomed to a miserable life.

Inspiring people to fear you will never make you as powerful as someone who can inspire others to love them. (See: Harry, Dumbledore.)

Attempting to rule through fear is always ultimately doomed/can never be ultimately successful.

So, there are several ways to find the theme of a story:

1) look for 'quotables';
2) look at the ending particularly to see if the theme is stated outright;
3) look at the difference between the characters at the beginning and the end;
4) look at the main characters' (plural) major failures;
5) look at the main characters' successes;

6) look for the lessons the 'bad characters' fail to learn.

Take any of these things, turn them into a full sentence that comments in some way on how we should live our lives, and ta da! You just identified a theme.

Now, if you're paying attention, you'll notice that any one of these methods will net you not just one, but a whole bunch of themes. So now let's head onwards, and talk about sub-themes. (Alternatively, if you need some more convincing that themes are even important, head to chapter eight, or if you're a writer and want to learn how all this applies to your own work, see chapter seven.)

CHAPTER SIX

Alright, you've got your head around the idea of a theme; now it's time to talk sub-themes. As you'll have noticed if you've been paying attention (which, if you're not, why are you reading this book right now?! Go sleep, or do something useful to reset your concentration meter!), every time we took one character or instance or quote and generated some themes from it, we did get themes—as in *some* themes, plural. This is the sticking point for people who don't 'get' English-style thinking, because this is the reason there's more than one right answer: because there's more than one theme.

Now, granted, some of you will be or have been stuck with English teachers who didn't let you have your own answer, and sometimes an answer *is* just plain wrong*. But on the whole, the point of a literary analysis is that *you* get to decide which theme is the most important *right now*—in reference to the question, absolutely, but also for you, as a human being.

A question asking you about power in Margaret Atwood's *The Handmaid's Tale*, for example, leaves you open to discuss any one of numerous thematic points she is making about power, and it's up to you to choose your focus and use it to respond to the question.

I had a university professor once who was fond of noting that Hamlet is not a muffin. This was his way of pointing out that, while there are many acceptable interpretations of a text, if you're contradicting its literal evidence then you can be flat-out wrong: Hamlet is not, in point of fact, a muffin.

This is why it can feel like the right answer is all in flux when it comes to theme in English. But actually, it's just a product of the fact that we, as humans, are really good at taking one situation with some other humans, and figuring out ways that they apply to our lives. It's a function of human interaction and society, the base necessity that we have to be able to learn from the actions and mistakes of others. As we've seen in previous chapters, one event = multiple themes, because our brains excel at making connections that suggest how we should live, because it wants to keep us alive.

Now, any given text is going to have some themes that are more prominent than others. The most prominent themes are going to be related to the journey of the most prominent character/s.

But when you figure that, in a well-written text, you should be able to trace a developmental journey for most of the minor characters as well, you can see how the number of themes in any given text can quickly spiral.

I mean, I wrote you an 800-word version of the *The Hare and The Tortoise* with essentially only two characters (the rest are mostly props, rather than actual characters), and I still got at least four themes straight off the top of my head there.

People. *Themes are everywhere.*

Now, there are two things a writer can do when it comes to subthemes. One is to ignore them entirely and just let them happen as they happen. This is a legit course of action, and is often actually advisable.

However, really good texts often have some next-level stuff going on with their subthemes.

You can tell when an author is in total control of the idea of themes, because not only will they have the main character exploring one particular set of themes/ideas, the minor characters' journeys will all speak to aspects of the same concept.

You might have a romance where the main character is learning to be herself and love who she is before she can find love from someone else; for the story to really hang together thematically, then, you could have the main male character exploring the opposite side of the coin: he loves himself so much he hasn't got emotional room left over for anyone else, so he has to learn to dial it down a little and not be an arrogant poo.

And then you could have the 'bad guy' failing to learn to care for other people, and a side character never learning to love themselves or make peace with who they are; another side character learning to love who they are and being okay with being single because at least now they're content with their own company; someone who's alone and bitter and never learns to be okay with themselves; et cetera et cetera, so on and so forth.

You get themes like:

It's important to accept yourself in order to live a fulfilling life.

You must accept yourself before others can accept you.

It's important to care for others in order to live a fulfilling life/find happiness.

It is both difficult and necessary to balance your own needs with the needs of others.

It's more important to love yourself than to find 'true love'. (This is from that minor character who learns to love themselves while being single.)

So you see, you have the one central idea (in this case, the importance of accepting yourself) embodied in your main character, and everyone else spirals around that, approaching that central idea from different directions.

You're going to end up with semi-random, unrelated themes too as natural consequences of whatever happens in your plot (say our romance heroine has to make the call whether or not to sell the family home, and now you're also looking at themes relating to memory, whether you need physical things in order to remember the past, whether holding onto things past their usefulness is nostalgic and sweet or weighing you down, etc), but the primary drive of each character's story is pointing in the same direction—and you end up with a magical story that feels super satisfying to the reader, because even if they don't realise this consciously, their subconscious (the bit that's expert at interpreting theme in order to survive) will definitely hear it, and will note that all characters point in the same direction, and will be Satisfied.

Subthemes: the literal icing on the thematic cake of story.

(Hmm, or is it that theme is sugar and you can just stick to using sugar in the main cake of your story—primary themes—but if you add some more as icing then you get a really amazing dessert? Look, something like that. You know what I mean. Onwards!)

CHAPTER SEVEN

So you're a writer, or a student who has to write a story for school or some such, and now you have an understanding of how theme works in other people's work and why it's important... but you're not really sure how to implement it in your own work, or what all this means for you.

That's okay: I'm here for you!

The first thing to bear in mind is that it's nearly impossible to write a good story with specific themes at the forefront of your mind. I'm sure it can be done, but generally speaking, if you're writing to a very *specific* theme, you're going to end up with a sermon poorly disguised as story, rather than an actual story.

Nobody reads a story to be preached at. Theme is important, foundational, and the reason that stories are valuable—but it's entirely incidental to the telling of the story. Theme is designed to hit us hard in the feels, and that doesn't work if it's blatant, unsophisticated, and/or too obvious—that just hits us right in the criticals, and no one appreciates being hit in the criticals.

So, if you're writing stories and want to introduce theme purposefully, what you're actually better off doing is reverting to that incorrect-but-generally-accepted definition of a 'theme' as a single word or phrase—a concept. Think about writing a story about 'love', rather than writing a story about 'Love is necessary in order to live a fulfilling life', or whatever. The actual, *specific* themes will develop through your characterisation (remember, it's impossible to write a story without a theme, even if you don't think about it deliberately), and you won't be tempted to veer into preaching territory.

Concepts. Stick to concepts.

And speaking of 'sticking', if you *are* going to look at theme in your own writing, something to watch out for is making sure that it's consistent throughout. You can pre-plan this or deal with it after (see below for options), but if there *is* a specific concept that you're aiming for, you need to make sure that a) you rely on it consistently throughout to b) inform the character's decisions.

If you want love to be a key concept in your story, the choices your character makes must be consistently related to love. And if you *do* want to make a particular statement *about* love, you'd best make sure your main character isn't making a key decision that contradicts what you think you're trying to say.

So. Onwards to look at your options for implementing all of this. Make sure to read all the sections below (please?), no matter what kind of writer you are. There's information in each section that is also generally useful and widely applicable.

FOR THE PLOTTERS

Ah, plotters. I understand, I do: it saves time to work the kinks out of the story when it's in outline form, rather than when you realise you've written 60,000 words in the wrong direction.

You feel in control.

You feel confident in your story.

It's efficient, because you're not writing so many wrong words, and when you sit down to write, you can skip most of the agony of trying to figure out what happens next. I get it. So how does theme fit into your plans?

Quite, quite easily. You can perform a thematic analysis of an outline just as easily as you can of an entire story! Look at your character's decisions and mistakes, their moments of despair and triumph, and just like we did in the early chapters here, figure out what message you're sending.

Check out your minor characters, and see if you have them pointing in similar directions to your main characters.

While you're outlining, figure out what your core concept is likely to be ('romantic love'; 'courage'; 'friendship'), and when faced with a decision about what a character should do or how a plot cog will fit, think about how you can make this decision relevant to that one central thematic idea that you're dealing with.

They don't *all* have to be, of course, but the more arrows you can point in the direction of your core concept, the more themes you're going to have that relate to each other, adding layers of depth to your work.

(It is probably possible to overdo this; stories are not, fundamentally, about preaching a point after all. So if it feels like it's starting to get too much, or too contrived, or too coincidental, feel free to back off a bit. Remember, the themes will be there whether you think about them or not.)

FOR THE PANSTERS*

So called because pantsers write 'by the seat of their pants', making it up as they go along, without an outline or a specific plan.

Pansters, exploratory writers, writers-into-the-dark: whichever name you call it by, for you, it's all about journeying into the unknown, letting your subconscious filter the story onto the page, surprising both your readers and yourself. It's like doing a giant jigsaw puzzle with only the vaguest glimpse of the picture on the box, at once scary or frustrating, and also elating.

If you're keen to introduce theme in a purposeful way into your writing, you have a couple of options, depending on exactly how you 'pants' your way through your writing. If you're a reviser, you can check for it afterwards in revision (see below).

If, on the other hand, you're a cycler (you revise as you go and end up with a basically finished story by the time you hit the end), you might be happy to know that you can build theme in exactly the same way you build story: piece by piece until you have a finished puzzle.

As you write, you'll start to get a sense of both who your main characters are, and what your major conflict is going to be. This should indicate to you some core concepts that your story is revolving around. As you make decisions about which piece of the jigsaw puzzle best fits next, you can start to consider the 'fit' of these pieces also by whether or not they align with the core concepts you've set up. And once you know what your ending is, you'll be able to figure out what some of your specific themes are—or what they might be, depending on the actions your character takes to get to that ending.

(Does your character save the puppy to get to the ending, or do they ditch the puppy to get to the ending? Different theme, depending on which one plays out best.)

You might also find that theme becomes a helpful way of spotting what the best jigsaw puzzle pieces will be: as you approach your ending and the range of possible options narrows, the options will narrow even further if you consider them through the lens of theme, or what point it is that you want to make about how humans should live.

Instead of just relying on plot and character to determine which jigsaw puzzle pieces you want, you're also now working with theme—something akin to knowing that you want the picture of the green leaves dancing in the wind, not the picture of the yellow ones. Same concept, different colour, but now you've figured out that you're building a puzzle of green leaves (which, depending on how many leaves there are in the picture, may have been easy to spot, or may have taken you weeks of piecing together all the sky bits before you realised the picture shows dancing leaves as well), you know you're safe to skip the yellow pieces, even if they're pretty.

FOR THE REWRITERS/REVISERS

This is actually where I find theme most handy myself. After I've written the story, I'll go back over it and as well as tracking things like character arcs and plot holes, I'll also note down any core concepts I can find and track these through the story, usually just with a bit of a colour code: scenes with a blue spot all deal with family relationships in some way, scenes with a yellow dot deal with feeling responsibility for the protection and welfare of other people. Et cetera.

It's simple, but can be a handy check when you're trying to decide whether you need to keep a scene or let it go. If it fits with your core concepts in some substantial way, you're probably good to keep it. If it doesn't touch on any of them, the scene is likely to feel disconnected from and/or irrelevant to the main story.

COUNTERPOINT FOR EVERYONE

Here's an intriguing counterpoint for you: You don't actually have to think about this at all! After all, you've written stories before, right? Guess what? They had themes! Congrats. You are officially a certified theme deployer.

Of course, if you want to make sure theme is working as hard as it can for you in stories, it's worth honing your skills—but that doesn't have to mean tying yourself in knots while you're writing the actual story. Your subconscious is just as clever as you are (sometimes a little cleverer, actually, I've found), and absorbs all the same information as your conscious, critical brain. So if you start paying attention to theme any time you see it around you (TV shows, movies, books: available everywhere stories are found!), you're actually training your subconscious to recognise theme as important.

The more time you devote to something, the more important it is, right?

Well, guess what? Your subconscious knows this. Start paying a lot of attention to theme, and your subconscious will get the message that you consider theme important. Your subconscious, being you, after all, wants to make you happy, so if you say theme is important, by golly, it's going to work hard to make sure theme works for you in your stories. I know, it sounds too easy, too vague. But I promise: it really does work.

Pay attention to theme. Trust your intuition when you're writing and something pops up, as this is often the subconscious signalling to you that there's a better, cleverer way to get to where you're going. Practice, and eventually you'll find that theme is working out in your stories just fine on its own.

If you want to get a sense of where you're at now, it can help to have someone who's good at and comfortable with the idea of theme look over something you've written and tell you what they think the themes are; you might be pleasantly surprised, and find that there's more thematic resonance in your stories than you thought, especially if you're at the stage where you're brave enough to sound like you on the page. If you're writing in your own, authentic voice, your values and philosophies are going to seep through into your writing (you know this, you've heard it before)—which means there are going to be themes there that you believe in, whether you meant to put them there or not.

Remember: just because you did something by accident doesn't mean you didn't do it.

PART TWO

Okay, so now you know how to find the theme of any story, and you're hopefully not quite so terrified of all this theme bizzo. There's still one thing I might need to convince you of though: Why does this actually matter? Who, apart from English teachers, actually cares about the theme of a text?

Well, for that, we're going to need to go on a quick tour of Stories Through History. Buckle up. It's going to be a fast and bumpy ride.

Storytelling has been around for at least as long as writing has, and given the centrality of oral storytelling in many cultures, it's safe to assume it's been around a lot longer than that.

The first *recorded* story that we have is the Epic of Gilgamesh, an epic written somewhere between 2150 and 1400 BC. It's a heroic tale from ancient Assyria complete with brave hero, horrible monsters to be slain, and a quest.

But why do we tell stories at all?

Basically, there are two theories when it comes to storytelling. One is that storytelling, like other art forms, is essentially just a meaningless by-product of human culture.

However, this fails to take into account the cost of creating art and telling stories: particularly in early hunter-gatherer societies, it doesn't seem sensible that someone would willingly choose to expend significant time and energy creating something that is essentially pointless, when most of their day would otherwise be taken up with activities that ensure survival.

And so we have the second theoretical camp, which suggests that there must be something intrinsically beneficial about creating art and telling stories, in order to make the effort expended on it worthwhile.

So what is this intrinsic benefit? What *does* make the act of storytelling and story consumption worthwhile?

As we'll see, research suggests that there are *several* key benefits:

- Stories draw on our ability to recognise and predict patterns to help us make sense of the world.
- Stories act as memory aids to encode information for easier retrieval later.
- Stories encourage cooperation and sociability.
- Stories and the telling thereof change or reinforce social hierarchies and power structures.
- Stories (of a particular kind) foster and develop empathy and our theory of mind.

So let's investigate each of these now in more detail.

CHAPTER EIGHT:
RECOGNISING PATTERNS

Human beings, particularly in a pre-industrial, pre-(western)scientific setting, live at the mercy of nature, which can often make life feel chaotic, random, and driven by chance. Although we like to think that our actions drive our successes, many times in life this isn't the case: we're blindsided by either good or bad fortune, our hands are forced, and life (or the actions of other people) makes our decisions for us.

Whether there actually *is* an underlying sense of logic and order in nature that's simply obscure sometimes, or whether humans simply require logic behind everything in order to satisfy our own intellectual needs, many stories (particularly from pre-industrial, pre-(western)scientific settings) focus on making sense of the world 'out there'.

Stories have a particular, predictable pattern of their own (which differs a little across cultures, time periods, genres and mode of telling—oral vs. written vs. staged vs. filmed, etc., but not as much as you might expect) and through them, we can impose patterns on what we see around us. It helps us feel in control and stabilised, to find patterns in lives that might otherwise seem chaotic and random, and ultimately helps us to convey these findings to others, in turn helping *them* to feel more secure as well (which has benefits for the social group as a whole, as well as for the individuals).

In fact, humans are so good at detecting patterns that we often see them even where they aren't: our habit of seeing faces in everything around us is one example of this, with the human brain so attuned to the importances of faces that it sees them everywhere, from the shape of a plug, to a passing cloud, to a stain on the floor, to a company logo.

This is just as true for stories. A well-known experiment tested this theory by showing participants a series of geometric shapes moving across a screen—some circles, triangles, etc. When asked to describe what they'd seen, almost every single participant responded in the form of a story, assigning emotions and intent to the geometric shapes they'd seen—transforming random movements into part of a pattern, or, more accurately, recognising that the random movements they were seeing actually fit a pre-defined pattern they already knew, a pattern that described a particular type of social interaction.

CHAPTER NINE: MEMORY AIDS

This idea of matching our observations to patterns we already know is actually a very important part of learning; in teacher training, for example, we're constantly reminded to link new content with something that students already know, to 'give them a hook to hang it on' or to contextualise it, so that students can see how it fits and thus remember it more easily. This makes sense: remembering one, random thing in isolation is a lot harder than remembering one new detail that fits in with a bunch of things you already know.

And of course, what is a story but a set sequence of events that you know and remember?! So matching external events to story patterns just makes sense. If you can match the random movement of some shapes on a screen to a familiar story pattern (in the case mentioned above, one of the triangles was frequently said to be chasing the other, smaller triangles, and the story-pattern surrounding domestic violence was repeatedly hinted at), then instead of having to remember random movements in isolation, you now have a story that you have already internalised to help you remember them.

In fact, estimates suggest that people remember information woven into stories up to *twenty-two times more effectively* than information provided through facts alone.

This is also why storytelling is such a popular component in many mnemonic techniques. If you want to improve your ability to memorise random lists of things (say, the items you're supposed to buy when you next hit up the grocery store), most of the well-known recommendations involve linking the items together in a story in some way. You could, for example, remember the list 'milk, stock powder, oranges, jam' by concocting a story like this one:

Once there was a small child who really, really liked to drink milk. *They liked it so much that even when they were banned from drinking* milk, *they would take it down to the* stock *yard so they could hide away and drink it in peace. Their favourite spot to hide in the* stock *yards was on the edge under the* orange *tree, where they could* jam *themselves in tightly between the rails and the tree trunk and drink* milk *in peace for hours on end.*

The link to 'jam' is a little more obscure than I'd like, but as an example in a book that is not about teaching mnemonic tricks, it'll do.

The point is that even in concocting this tiny, three-sentence example, I couldn't help myself: I turned it into a real story. This was not pre-planned in any way, shape or form; I literally just invented this as I was typing it. And yet, I have a character, in a specific setting, with a clearly defined goal, and some conflict—there's the child, in some kind of rural or semi-rural setting, who really, really wants to drink milk, but has to hide in order to do so because they're banned from it.

(Maybe they have an intolerance, I don't even know. Also, why you'd put an orange tree right next to your stock yard is beyond me. BUT NEVER MIND. It's a shopping list, not a candidate for the Nobel Prize.)

Storytelling as a memory aid also has much more significant cultural implications than mnemonic tricks and shopping lists. People are significantly more likely to remember things and be impacted by them when they understand them both intellectually *and* emotionally, so if I simply tell my child not to play with chainsaws, that's one thing, but if I tell them not to *and* tell them that they could get hurt *and* show them the pictures of my friend's knee when he nearly severed his own leg off in a chainsaw accident? Yeah, whole lot more effective.

(And no, I haven't traumatised my children, I promise. Well, not yet, anyway.)

(This is also why ads, both of the commercial variety and the 'save a child' social-issue variety, are careful to include an emotional pull, as well as mere intellectual information.)

This concept of passing important factual information via stories is illustrated clearly in the Indigenous Australian concept of songlines. A songline is a particular story or set of stories that is connected to physical locations within the people's geographic area, and while the stories hold immense religious and cultural significance, they also expertly convey the factual information necessary to survive in that area: the location of seasonal water and food, to name just one example. And in an awe-inspiring example of the social currency of stories, many of these songlines are connected from culture to culture, over-arching narratives with individual chapters, with each culture the curators of the particular 'chapter' of the story relevant to their land.

CHAPTER TEN: SOCIAL COOPERATION

Which segues nicely into our third point: that stories foster social cooperation.

The act of telling a story implies an audience, someone to have the story told to, especially in the case of oral storytelling. And there's a reason that parents are encouraged to read to their children: the act of storytelling is bonding, reinforcing the relationship first between both story tellers and story-consumers, and secondly between all the various story-consumers together (I mean, witness the fan-led forums online where people bond fiercely over their favourite books, movies and TV shows—a perfect example of storytelling creating bonds and group identity).

This is also where you see the power story has over groups with a shared story-background; not only do you get passionate fandoms, you get things which are conceptually similar but on a larger scale: patriotism, after all, is simply a shared story about how wonderful our own corner of the world is, and an invested belief in it being better than other corners of the world. Democracy, freedom, equality—these are not physical, absolute *things*, but rather values that arise out of a shared narrative. We tell each other stories about how things matter, how they make the world a better place, and if we tell these stories often enough, and the people in power tell them enough, the concepts they embody become a reality. A shared cultural narrative—a common set of stories you tell yourself about who you are like, and who you are not like—is one of the key traits of group belonging, whether that group is a *Harry Potter* fan club or the United States of America.

I can attest personally to the power of this kind of storytelling: my son is of an age where he is noticing that other people sometimes choose to do things that we encourage him not to do, or that we just happen to not do in our house.

An easy example: we're vegetarian. A lot of our extended family is, but not all of them, and certainly most of his friends at school are not. And the simplest explanation for him is, some families choose to do things differently. Some families choose to eat meat, and that's fine. It's just that in our family, we choose not to.

You'd think this would be on par with 'Because I said so' as reasoning goes, but this is where we see the subtle, yet persuasive, power of stories: we are *not* saying 'Do this things for no reason'. Instead, we are suggesting (and this was totally unintentional at the time!) that in order to belong, in order to be a part of our family, this is the story we tell: that we do not eat meat. And so, because there is the hint of a story attached, a story that describes the members of our family group, he seems to have not only accepted it unquestioningly, but (to my utter embarrassment) also to have become one of those militant vegetarians who proudly informs all his friends, *Well*, we *don't do that in* our *family!*

I mean, it's embarrassing as heck sometimes, but it shows clearly the power of a shared narrative in forming group identity and cooperation between group members, right?

(Pity about the conflict between non-group members...!)

On a broader scale, religion serves a similar purpose, particularly in post-agricultural societies: as well as linking back to that idea of providing patterns in chaos and thus meaning in our lives, religion also functions as a way of ensuring social harmony (again, as with the example of my son, at least *within* the group) by telling stories that convey a shared set of expectations for behaviour.

In hunter-gatherer societies, we can see clearly how stories perform this role of maintaining social harmony: in studies conducted into the cultural stories of hunter-gatherer societies across southeast Asia and Africa, anthropologists found that around 70% of stories specifically concern social behaviour, implicitly conveying the social rules around hunting, sharing food, marriage, and interactions with members of other groups.

Some anthropologists suggest that it's important for groups to share stories like this not just because it lets us know how we should act, but also because it means we can rest assured knowing that other people know the same set of social rules as we do.

If we know that someone belongs to the same religion, or meet someone of our own nationality while overseas, or discover someone has a similar physical condition to us, we instantly know that they 'get it'—that they understand some of the rules by which we operate and through which we frame the world. We can rest easier, knowing that a shared set of stories has done the heavy lifting for us in defining the way we should interact.

CHAPTER ELEVEN: SOCIAL/POWER STRUCTURES

In all of this, there may be some interesting things going on with our background psychology. Some monkey scientists (as in scientists who study monkeys, not, you know, unusually inquiring and intellectual monkeys) have suggested that when monkeys groom each other, it's not actually primarily about hygiene and keeping parasites/pests down after all: the act of grooming, they suggest, plays an important social role because there seem to be interesting 'rules' at play about who gets to groom whom and for how long—the more important you are, the more grooming you attract.

Basically, this act of grooming has been equated to a form of social monkey gossip—and about two-thirds of human communication is thought to be gossip, not necessarily in the negative, stigmatised sense, but in the sense of telling stories about what other people are doing.

Think about that for a second. Up to two-thirds of all human communication is us telling each other stories about what we and other people are doing. That's a lot of stories being used every day as social glue, to keep us connected and informed about each other.

Of course, the other function of gossip, beyond conveying facts and linking us with those around us, is navigating power. Sometimes 'gossip', or stories about real people, can be used to challenge existing power structures or hierarchies, and sometimes it can be used to reinforce it. Likewise, stories in general have the same ability to either challenge or affirm existing power structures.

This is because, like it or not, storytelling seems to hold a position of power in human society.

To test this theory, researchers sought out populations in south-east Asia and assessed them both for the number of esteemed storytellers they contained, and also the degree of cooperation displayed by the population.

The camps that had a greater number of esteemed storytellers were indeed found to be more cooperative overall. Additionally, these storytellers weren't lubricating the wheels of society without any benefit to themselves: storytellers were found throughout the various populations surveyed to be preferred social partners, and to be more likely to be the recipient of shared food.

As a flow-on benefit from this, they were found to have on average an additional 0.5 surviving children compared to non-storytellers.

Now, this is only one study, and the researchers themselves noted that further longitudinal studies would be needed to really affirm these findings, but it does at least strongly suggest that storytellers hold a position of power in society. This doesn't just apply to hunter-gatherer societies, of course: check out any A-list of celebrities in the contemporary western world and you'll find it chock full of people whose job it is to tell stories, whether that be through writing them, acting them, or telling them through other means ('a day in the life of' reality-style TV, anyone? That's just another kind of gossip story!).

We've known throughout history how powerful stories can be; that's why the printing press was such a disruptive piece of technology. Not only did it make stories in general accessible to the public, it made the *special* ones, the religious ones, things that could no longer be controlled by a small group of powerful people—and by making these stories public, it took away some of the power from the people who, previously, had been the storytellers.

If you're still feeling skeptical about the power of stories, you just have to look at the history of storytelling technology, and how it was received by society at the time of its invention. It's not just the printing press that was considered highly disruptive to polite society: literally every development in the way stories are told to the public was initially decried as a horrible, immoral, and corrupting.

The invention of the novel was derided as a lewd and inappropriate use of one's time. Then, with the improvement of printing presses and cheap paper, as well as access to cheaper distribution, came serialisation: the release of stories one chapter at a time in magazine, periodicals, or even as cheap-quality paperbacks in their own right. The outcry over this was even more vocal, with detractors commenting that this was 'not the right way' to indulge in reading, as it wasn't a 'mere healthy recreation' like cricket, conversation or back-gammon.

Serial reading, people: Not A Healthy Recreation.

Then of course came movies and television, still today considered 'lower' forms of storytelling by much of society (if only because we haven't per-fected the next wave of storytelling technology yet).

Huxley made his opinions on these new 'talkies' clear, with John the Savage in *Brave New World* recoiling in disgust at the 'feelies' he is taken to see.

Bradbury was similarly scathing of the television, shown clearly in his novel *Fahrenheit 451*, where the installation of large, window-sized screens (which are essentially TVs showing soap operas) has stripped the population of its will to learn anything.

See also the various 'banned books' movements throughout history, which have sought to remove from public circulation reading material that they felt encouraged negative behaviour—in many cases, code for 'challenged existing social narratives'.

Stories clearly have power, or we wouldn't be afraid of them.

CHAPTER TWELVE:
EMPATHY

Strangely, though, what it seems that stories *most* have the power to do is make us better people. It's true that stories, particularly group narratives, can have tremendously negative impacts (consider the stories told by racist hate groups, for example), but stories also have the power to shape society for the better.

Despite the continued existence of some detractors (who, I can only imagine, are either not big readers themselves, or else are reading mostly books with themes that encourage them to become worse versions of who they are), a wide range of studies have shown pretty convincingly that consuming stories—reading, in particular, sorry to disappoint—actually makes us more understanding of others, more empathetic, and generally better-quality human beings.

There's a trick here, though: the kind of story you consume matters.

Generally speaking, when we say that consuming stories can make you a better person, we're talking about narratives, actual stories with characters and a beginning, a middle and an end.

Narrative non-fiction certainly exists (memoirs, biographies, etc.), and we are probably fairly safe to assume that the generalisations made about fiction apply to narrative non-fiction as well… but generally the research deals more simply with just 'fiction' and 'non-fiction'.

So, when I say that stories have the power to make us better people, the research suggests I'm talking about fiction specifically: made-up stories about events that didn't actually happen in the real world exactly as they're stated, stories told through the lens of a particular and identifiable character.

So what can consuming fiction do for our souls?

Generally speaking, consuming fiction is a great way to develop our 'theory of mind'. A 'theory of mind' (sometimes capitalised as Theory of Mind) is the ability we have to recognise that other people think different thoughts to ourselves; our inner life is not the inner life of every person we meet.

Consuming fiction is known to help develop this ability because it gives us practice in observing how people other than us think in a close, intimate way not usually possible with regular people (look, I know I talk to myself a lot, but if you sat in a room listening to me, you still wouldn't be getting the same kind of access to my inner thoughts as you would if I were a character in a story).

This brings us to the first important point: sorry, everyone, but reading really is superior to other ways of consuming stories in this particular aspect, if only because of our storytelling conventions. In visual media, it's hard to be 'in the head' of the character we're following; it's cheesy and unrealistic to have a movie full of voiceovers giving us the character's thoughts and inner monologue.

In books, on the other hand, this is all perfectly acceptable. We're used to seeing the character's thoughts written there on the page, as though we had a magical little connection directly with their brain.

So reading fictional stories can improve our theory of mind. What else can it do?

A 2014 study found that reading fiction generally (as opposed to reading non-fiction) lowered racial bias: after reading the stories provided to them, participants were less likely to assign random photos of racially-ambiguous faces to particular races based solely on their facial expressions (before reading, there'd been a distinct correlation between the face showing a negative emotion, and the participant labelling it as not-the-same-race-as-themselves). After reading the stories, people were more likely to see similarities between 'people like themselves' and 'people like the ones in the story'.

They were also more likely to behave empathetically in real-life situations, such as when the researcher "accidentally" dropped a handful of pens nearby. (The participants who reported being 'highly absorbed' in the story were about two times more likely to help than participants who reported not being particularly engaged with the story /stories they'd read.)

So this is the next key point: we need to be 'highly absorbed' with what we're reading. This is because of what I mentioned before about knowing something intellectually *and* knowing it emotionally: if you're just skimming, you're absorbing the story only on an intellectual level, rather than engaging emotionally with it.

(And look, I know it's really, really hard to engage emotionally with something if you're a slow reader. I'm genuinely sad to report that I don't have a solution here, except to say that, as with any other skill, practice really can improve your reading speed.)

And finally, a 2013 study wanted to investigate for-realsies whether some types of books increase empathy better than others, and what they found is that books that are all about the interior narrative of the character, all about experiencing the world the way someone else does, promote empathy best. (Totally shocking, right?)

Books that don't seek to promote the interior life of the characters have little to no impact on the reader's natural levels of empathy.

(The way the researchers said it was that literary stories promote empathy better than popular fiction or non-fiction, but given their definition of 'literary stories' was 'narratives that focus on in-depth portrayals of subjects' inner feelings and thoughts, I think us genre fans can rest assured that there are plenty of 'literary' offerings in the genres we love as well—romance and a lot of young adult stories are often quite 'interior' as well.)

This all seems nicely logical, of course, so well done them for proving it with science.

So what, exactly, does all this have to do with theme? Okay, I've made a case for the important of stories in general, and hopefully convinced you that they hold an important place in society—but why does that discussion belong in a book on theme?

Look, if you've been following along closely, you already know the answer: because the meaning we derive from a story, the lessons we learn from it, *are* the themes. While elements of a plot can be twisty, fundamentally, there are a limited number of plots. While elements of setting can be incredibly cool, the concept of a space whale isn't going to change the way we live our lives. And while characters can be just as awesome as real, live human beings, it's what these characters learn, how they change and grow, what they overcome and how they triumph that stays with us—and as you now know, that's the entire basis of theme.

Stories tell us where we've come from; stories tell us who we are; and stories tell us who it's possible to be. In short, stories give us our identity, forging a sense of belonging, and creating meaning in our lives. And they do this because of theme.

PART THREE

Congratulations! You've survived this crash course in How To Theme :) If you're feeling a bit Done, feel free to tap out now. However, if you're up for one last little adventure, come with me now as we explore some of the major themes in a variety of common genres.

Themes are actually really important to writing successfully in genres—in fact, they're one of the main things that audiences are after when they turn to a particular genre of story. If you're feeling like a romance, you're likely looking for a fundamentally optimistic story about a relationship with a happy ending—as you'll see in the next chapter, this speaks directly to the range of possible themes in romance.

If you're after a mystery, it's probable that you're in need of a story that reminds you of the primacy of logic and order in an apparently-chaotic world— again, key thematic concepts in the genre, there because of the fact that the detective (professional or amateur) must *solve* the mystery.

In fact, it's probable that if we were psychologists, we could conduct some sort of personality analysis here and link particular personal values with genre preferences, because you're much more likely to consume stories (in any form, remember) that affirm your own life perspective than you are to seek out stories that challenge how you see the world (which, by the way, can be a highly rewarding experience, and I recommend doing it at least every now and then).

So, join me now on our extremely brief tour of a handful of major genres as we explore the themes that give these genres their identity.

CHAPTER THIRTEEN: ROMANCE

We're going to start with romance now in our look into genres. Why romance? Because romance is the only genre that has prescriptions about both the ending (must be happy for the main couple, otherwise it's a story with 'romantic elements', not a romance) *and* the characters (they must form an intimate relationship with each other, and the act of doing so must be a significant part of the plot).

Why is this important when we're talking about theme?

If you shouted enthusiastically across the room, "Because the themes are determined by the ending and the characters!", give yourself ten points and a pat on the back. (Fine, you can have ten points if you only *thought* this answer as well.)

Yes. Theme is determined by the way the characters end, so a genre with a prescribed ending is going to have a whole bunch of set or prescribed themes. How conveniently easy for us!

Romance is all about relationships, right: main character one meets main character two, often in a way that is offbeat and/or quirky, sparks fly (at least eventually they do, anyway), and by the end, the two main characters are 'together', at least for now. (That's actually an official distinction in the genre:

you have your stories where the characters get a HEA, a Happily Ever After, and you have your stories where they get a HFN, or Happily For Now. Either is acceptable—but these are the *only* acceptable endings in genre romance.)

So obviously, a lot of our themes are going to revolve around the importance of relationships, of finding a partner.

True love not only exists, it's worth fighting for.

If you close yourself off to the possibility of love, you're condemning yourself to live but a half life.

There's someone out there for everyone.

True love conquers all odds.

The right partner helps you be a better you.

Romance books are also, by and large, by women, about women, for women. Not always; I've read some great romance written by men about men, but much, much more frequently than not, you're going to get a book about a woman in romance. So we're going to expect some themes about the societal role of women as well—and if you're expecting them to all revolve around women needing to give up their hopes and dreams for the love of their life, you probably actually haven't read much romance! The romance genre, on the whole, is pretty progressive, being mostly penned as it is by women who, you know, write for a living. ;)

You are not defined by what society thinks of you.

Women have intrinsic value as human beings.

Everyone deserves respect.

You shouldn't have to give up on who you are as a person in order to make a relationship work.

(And, all real relationships involve compromise.)

And remember, because of that prescribed happy ending, the genre is ultimately hopeful and optimistic about human nature. Whereas something like old-school science fiction is often inherently pessimistic, because the purpose of it was to warn humanity of the dire things that could happen if science and technology got away from them, romance reassures us that happy endings are not only possible, they're plausible, too.

In a world of heartache and divorce, domestic violence, abuse, rape, and even very real sexual slavery trades, an entire genre dedicated to reminding us of all that's good and true and lovely about intimate human relationships plays an important role in shaping our perception of possibilities.

True love is possible and worth fighting for.

No matter bad things get, if you're with the right person, you'll pull through.

Somebody always loves you.

If it's not okay, it's not the end.

CHAPTER FOURTEEN: YOUNG ADULT

Personally, I think 'young adult' is more of a category, really, than a genre, but here we are. And despite the fact that 'young adult' can incorporate romance, science fiction, fantasy, mystery, historicals, and just about every other genre you can think of, there *are* definite similarities across the 'genre' itself, so fine: I'll stick to calling it a genre.

Fundamentally, young adult stories are targeted at people aged twelve-ish to eighteen-ish (hence the name, right). During this period of life, people are often shifting and growing and changing and developing in a more personal and intense way than during other periods in their lives—much like characters in stories. How helpful!

We know from earlier chapters that it's the change in our characters from the beginning of the story to the end that indicate the themes, and we know that young people change quite a bit (or consolidate themselves, if you prefer, rather than 'changing') during this time period... You can see where I'm going with this, right? We literally do not actually even need to look at any stories to predict (accurately) what the themes are likely to be, because Real Life People are handily fulfilling the role of characters here for us.

So what kind of changes or developments in character are common (not universal, mind, just common) during this period of life?

Generally, this is the age...

- where people are developing an extended awareness of the world beyond their own experiences;
- where romantic relationships and sexuality become a Thing;
- where empathy for others and other ways of living is developing;
- where people begin to either consolidate themselves as part of their childhood families, or separate and forge their own identity (or, more usually, parts of both);
- where you might be confronted with good friends making decisions based on a different set of morals than your own;
- where you're living in a highly-artificial environment for the majority of your weekly hours (i.e. school) (and I don't necessarily mean 'artificial' as negative, just that school is a lot more human-constructed and micro-managed than most environments you encounter as an adult);
- that adults aren't magical unicorns who have all their rainbow-coloured poop together every moment of every day;
- where gaining responsibility also means gaining the opportunity to royally screw up...

...and so forth.

Let's pull some possible themes out of that, bearing in mind that *themes are determined by the ending of the story*—so if someone has a happy conclusion to their teen years, you're going to get optimistic themes, while if they have negative experiences that continue to have negative impacts on them through their 'new adult' years, you've essentially got a 'sad ending' to the teenage period, and you'll have fundamentally pessimistic themes.

It's important to consider other people's world views.

Other people live by different sets of morals, and sometimes this is okay, and sometimes it's not, and trying to figure out where that line sits is a difficult and necessary and constantly-shifting life challenge.

One person's experiences are not universal.

One person's problems can feel like the end of the world.

One person's problems can be the end of the world.

Young people can do amazing things.

Young people are not absolved of the responsibility to act like good humans just because they are young.

Adults aren't magically moral human beings just because they're adults.

Growing up doesn't necessarily mean getting wiser.

Sexuality is a normal and important part of an individual's identity.

Intimate relationships are necessary but complicated.

Family is what you make of it.

Family makes you who you are; you make you who you will be.

Family are the people who are always there for you.

(Deliberately ambiguous.)

You are more like your parents than you thought.

Everyone will let you down eventually.

Horrible people might win at teenage-dom, but they usually end up losing at life.

Be yourself.

It's important to learn to love who you are.

Gaining freedoms means gaining responsibilities.

Gaining responsibilities means gaining opportunities to royally screw up.

I could keep going, but you know what? You get the point. If you want some homework, here:

Think of at least three more themes broadly applicable to young adults and their stories. I'm sure it'll take you all of about three minutes ;)

CHAPTER FIFTEEN: FANTASY

Central to the fantasy genre is the idea of a 'sense of wonder', a semi-technical term referring to the ability such stories have to inspire in us a sense of awe at a world far larger than ourselves, at the possibilities of the universe, at the wonders of the imagination.

Often, this takes the form of something 'magic' in the story (whether or not the characters acknowledge it as or call it 'magic' is irrelevant), be that some sort of force that characters can tap into or manipulate, or fantastical creatures, or just a situation out of the ordinary. Sometimes a story will try to explain the mechanics behind this awe-inspiring device, and sometimes it will be left entirely unexplained, for the reader to simply accept or not. But because of this, there are a raft of themes we can immediately spot:

The supernatural/paranormal/spiritual is not only real, it is integral to our understanding of ourselves.

Human beings can and should strive to be more.

The visible, tangible world is not the be-all and end-all.

There's more to life than meets the eyes.

The supernatural/paranormal/spiritual is accessible to at least some human beings and enriches the lives of those who touch it.

You'll note here that one of the alternative terms included here is 'spiritual'. Please note that I say this from the position of being a pretty religious person myself:

Yes, in the context of a literary analysis, a lot of religious texts belong to the 'fantasy' genre, not because I am implying that they are untrue, unrealistic, or un-anything else, but simply because they deal with the supernatural.

This is not just an arbitrary grouping; it actually has a relatively significant impact on the themes you can expect to find in the fantasy genre, because many of our most well-known fairytales and fantasy tropes have their roots in (various) religion(s); similarly, many of the ethical and moral preoccupations of the fantasy genre also have their roots in religion.

This preoccupation with the supernatural also creates a natural power imbalance to explore: if you have some people who can control magic, you have others who cannot; if you have supernatural beings, you have 'normal' people too. Hence, we get extremely common themes such as:

Good will ultimately triumph over evil.

It's our ethics and morality that make us human rather than our skills and abilities.

Power corrupts, and absolute power corrupts absolutely.

With great power comes great responsibility.

The degree of power we wield is not our defining trait.

Supernatural abilities can isolate us from mainstream

humanity; we can be more powerful than others or equal to them, but rarely both.

Another key element of fantasy is the ability to explore people unlike ourselves in a very literal, tangible way. We can explore issues such as racism, sexism, colonisation and other 'big' cultural issues at arm's length, depersonalising/de-emotionalising the issue and making it easier and more accessible to understand. Because of this, you find common themes such as:

All people are not alike, but all people deserve respect.

Enslaving magical creatures to do our bidding usually ends badly.

Creatures different from ourselves should be approached with respect, lest they turn out to be a lot more powerful than they first appeared.

Difference evokes fear, but actions driven by fear fairly inevitably end poorly.

Fantasy's other strong point is in the literalisation of humanity's fears, anxieties and emotions. Fantasy is, on at least some level (more or less depending on the subgenre), metaphor made real: the monster in the closet given a visible form; intangible horrors such as depression and anxiety made physical; society's greed or violence turned into a literal monster.

There's an appealing logic behind this: If something is physical, it's much easier to fight (or even just deal with, or make peace with).

Even the worst monsters can be slain.

Sometimes it's better to make friends with the monster than to fight it.

Even the most terrifying beasts have a weakness.

Greed (or violence, or…) can destroy a society.

CHAPTER SIXTEEN:
SCIENCE FICTION

Science fiction is, of course, stories that revolve around science and/or technology. In more contemporary stories, it's common enough to simply include a piece of advanced, mostly-plausible technology and call the resultant story 'science fiction', but at its heart, science fiction is more than simply trimmings: it's a genre that lives to question the very purpose of the science and technology that make the genre possible. Science fiction isn't just about what we *can* do, but about what we *should* do; it's about the ethics and morals behind the gadgets, about the social impacts of the discoveries.

Because 'science' is as broad and all-encompassing as life itself, there are a huge number of key concepts that science fiction deals with on a regular basis—and because science fiction is generally about ethics and morals, it's usually about the questions that those concepts raise.

Mind-hacking, space exploration, time travel: these raise questions about colonisation, individual rights, privacy, the nature of choice and free will.

Subgenres like SFR (science fiction romance) explore human relationships in science fiction settings, something that raises a different set of questions again.

Then there's the superhero subgenre, which addresses questions surrounding human nature, what super-humans would be like, what 'super' actually is, and suggests the need for good to fight against evil.

Aliens, A.I., cloning, technology, politics, post-apocalyptic worlds—all of these suggest questions surrounding the nature of humanity, the way in which we treat the Other, what happens when the enslaved become the slavers or the slavers become the enslaved, how far is too far when it comes to technology, what it means to be intelligent, what would happen if we discovered and/or created intelligence greater than our own, what the definition of 'artificial' actually is, and the limits of science, both possible and moral.

Remember, though, that it's what the text says *about* any of these things that are the themes. If a text was all about A.I. taking over the world and despising humanity because of how we'd treated it, the text would obviously be suggesting that a) creating intelligence greater than ourselves is a risky proposition, and b) we should be nice to the things (intelligences, people, creatures) below us, because one day they might be above us—or to invert that, it would be suggesting that oppressed slaves become oppressive masters.

Themes are full sentences; do not forget this.

Science fiction might be expansive, covering everything from gender and sexuality to time travel to wish-fulfillment devices bordering on the magical, but there are nevertheless some common themes. Some of the more familiar/common ones include:

Memory and emotional experience is somehow integral to the experience of being human. (*Blade Runner*)

Knowledge and learning are essential for fulfilment and life satisfaction. (*Fahrenheit 451*)

Everyone deserves fundamental dignity (usually including clones and artificial intelligences). (Take your pick! *Gattaca* is a commonly studied example. *Never Let Me Go* is a more contemporary example.)

Science and technology have both the capacity for great good and, in the wrong hands, for great evil. (Again, super common. *Jurassic Park*, to name one.)

Scientific exploration should seek to do no harm. (*Star Trek*)

Interfering with the natural course of things is a Really Bad Idea. (*Back To The Future*)

Good should triumph over evil. (Nearly every superhero story ever.)

The strong should protect the weak. (Ditto.)

Remember: science fiction is about questioning the logical possibilities of our world and about digging past what we technically *can* do to explore whether or not we *should* do it; it's fundamentally a genre based on the philosophy of ethics and morality.

CHAPTER SEVENTEEN: MYSTERY

Mystery, in all its varying forms, is fundamentally about the triumph of logic. It's one of the only genres that has a prescribed ending:

No matter what happens, no matter how convoluted or twisted the plot, the main character will *always* win out, solving the mystery to figure out what happened, and how, and why.

Hopefully you can see right away that this makes mystery also a fundamentally-optimistic genre!

The mystery can be crime-related (a murder, a theft, etc.) or simply something mysterious (What is the real story of the strange lady who lives in the house on the corner of the street?), and the detective figure can be a grizzled, cynical professional (hardboiled mysteries) or a grandmotherly woman (cozy mysteries), but the fundamental necessity for the mystery to be both solved by the character and solvable by the reader (at least in hindsight), means that the genre is speaking to the value of order over chaos, logic over randomness, the virtues of curiosity and observant-ness, and the importance of not leaping to conclusions (especially where red herrings are concerned).

So what are some key themes we can pull out from this?

(I expect you already have a good idea of what they will be based on what I've said here...)

All actions are fundamentally logical to the person who commits them.

Good always triumphs over evil.

Even the cleverest evil masterminds make mistakes which can catch them out.

It's important to follow your instinct.

Order trumps chaos.

Curiosity is a valuable asset in life.

People who are highly observant will discover things that 'ordinary' people cannot.

Everything happens for a reason.

Life is inherently logical.

Every mystery can be solved.

In subgenres like the police procedural, there's an additional layer of commentary, suggesting that authority figures in particular win out over chaos and evil, that the police are fundamentally good and on the side of 'the people', and—due to the common trope of the police detective figure as overworked and underpaid, the meat in the sandwich of hierarchy—there's also the suggestion that this detective figure in some way represents the 'every man'—every other person in the world who *also* feels overworked and underpaid, and suffers from being hierarchical meat in their place of work. So, to thematise:

Authority is fundamentally on the side of good.

Authorities will and ought to triumph over commoners

(usually common criminals).

Evil is usually better funded than good, but good can always be cleverer.

Using your head is more important than how many resources you have available.

Good people will rarely get the recognition they deserve, but will continue to work hard anyway.

Good people are good because *they work hard/do a good job despite poor resources and lack of recognition.*

Cozy mysteries, on the other hand, present us with a common, ordinary person in a different way, and suggest that everyone can make a difference and/or solve the mystery if they are persistent and observant enough.

Everyone can be a hero.

Everyone can make a difference.

Street smarts are more important than professional credits.

Persistence wins out in the end.

You don't need a formal qualification to beat the bad guys, you just need to be observant and persistent.

CONCLUSION

Theme.

Hopefully, now that you've read this book, it's no longer the scary or confusing word it once was. You know what a theme is (the point that a story is making about how we should live our lives), you know where and how to find it (at the end of the story and by figuring out how and why the characters changed, or failed to change), you know why it's important (because stories are how we learn how to human), you know how to implement it in your own writing (by teaching your sub-conscious to pay attention to it, and through the characterisation decisions you make), and you know what some of the key themes are likely to be for a bunch of popular genres.

My friend, you are Well Equipped now to navigate theme. Congratulations.

If you have any lingering questions or doubts, you're welcome to contact me!

The most reliable way to reach me is Twitter, where I'm @InkyLaurens. There are also a bunch of other places you can find me, all listed on my website, www.amylaurens.com.

The early chapters of this book are also posted there (look for the tag 'How To Theme') and you can comment and/or ask questions on most of those posts.

And so:

Go forth, noble human, and thematise!

Which is no more or less than saying, Go forth, noble human, and continue to learn through stories about what it means to be human, how to navigate this sticky situation we call life, how to be more, be better, be fulfilled, how to survive, to cope, to live… and just maybe, write stories that in turn show others how to human.

You're going to do an amazing job. *I believe in you. You got this.*

<3
A

REFERENCES

Bond, Sue. (2009). "Review - On the Origin of Stories". *Genetics and Evolution*. 13:41.

Delistraty, Cody C. (2014.) "The Psychological Comfort of Storytelling". *The Atlantic*. 2 November.

Deresiewics, Willian. (2014.) "How the Novel Made the Modern World". *The Atlantic*. June.

Gopnik, Adam. (2012). "Can Science Explain Why We Tell Stories?" *The New Yorker*. 18 May.

Johnson, Dan R., Huffman, Brandie L. & Jasper, Danny, M. (2014). "Changing Race Boundary Perception by Reading Narrative Fiction". *Basic and Applied Social Psychology*. 36:1(83-90).

Kidd, David Comer & Castano, Emanuele. (2013). "Reading Literary Fiction Improves Theory of Mind". *Science*. 342:6156(377-380).

Kluger, Jeffrey. (2017). "How Telling Stories Makes Us Human". *Time*. 5 December.

Rose, Frank. (2011). "*The Art of Immersion* Excerpt: Fear of Fiction". *Wired: Business*. 3 October.

Smith, Daniel. (2017). "Why Do We Tell Stories? Hunter-Gatherers Shed Light on the Evolutionary Roots of Fiction". *The Conversation*. 6 December.

Smith, Daniel, Schlepper, Philip & Major, Katie, et. al. (2017). "Cooperation and the Evolution of Hunter-Gatherer Storytelling." Nature Communications. 8 (1853).

EBOOK

Thank you for buying this book!

When you buy an Inkprint Press book in print, we like to thank you by offering you the ebook for free. Please head to:

http://www.inkprintpress.com/books/books-by-genre/non-fiction/how-to-theme/

and use the coupon THEMEPRINT to download your free copy in both .mobi and .epub formats.

ACKNOWLEDGEMENTS

With thanks to Krista for asking the questions that prompted this book, my amazing Patreon supporters for their feedback on my initial ideas, and Anthea for assistance with proofreading.

SUPPORTERS

With thanks to my amazing Patreon supporters, Clare, Thea and Bethy <3

https://www.patreon.com/amylaurens

ABOUT THE AUTHOR

AMY LAURENS is secretly a superhero.

HA! She wishes! That would definitely make it easier to get done the epic number of things on her daily to-do list.

Instead, she's actually just an ordinary person who happens to be pretty good at organising. Being a high-school teacher, a mum, a multi-small business owner, and somewhat of a habitual over-achiever will kind of do that to you.

Either that, or it will break you. Amy's been there done that too. On balance, she recommends hyper-organisation as a life strategy, compared to monthly breakdowns.

Or, you know, you could just not try to be amazing at everything all at once. That's probably the more sensible option.

…Sensible people never have any fun.

You can contact Amy at:
amyllaurens@gmail.com
www.amylaurens.com
https://www.patreon.com/amylaurens

www.ingramcontent.com/pod-product-compliance
Lightning Source LLC
Chambersburg PA
CBHW051031030426
42336CB00015B/2817